LOVE IS CURE

RASHI MEHRA

Contents

Preface

All the incidents that took place in this book are true also all the emotions of the book are true…

The names, places and circumstances differ slightly…

When you get the love you give you are lucky but when you don't and you still give all the love you have you are luckiest …very few amongst us are willing to do that…

Only love can give you the power of giving and giving and never being empty…

My plans in life were very different from this but I always knew my love for writing is never ending…

Be it in poems or stories …love made it all happen!

Prologue

Love is not about the years that you share it's about the moments you live in it…love is a crazy ride into the madness of your own soul…

A true lover can always recognize true love stories and this one is for all those who truly had the honor of being love…

Because we do not fall in love we somehow rise in it…true love gives you the strength to fight what you thought you're not capable enough to… and sometimes in the weakest moments of your life, true love memories give you the push you need to go on…

Like any other love story, this one too is all about "love"…

Can you be in love with someone long after they have left?

Can you be loyal towards your love long after they have left?

You can only know how deeply you are in love when you do not have the one you love around to share the same…

Will, they ever get a chance to be together?

Find out what happens to Angie and Keith's story…

Because the only thing that is constant is "love"

1. I. LOVE AS IT MAY SEEM

It all starts and ends with love - that's what she had in her mind all the time. It was a cozy winter evening; she had a glass of rose wine in one hand and remote of the television which she wasn't concentrating on. It

was almost a habitual thing about her every day when she turned up at her lonely house. Switching on the TV -changing channels and not remembering the content of the last one… then going back to where it

started finally ending up on a channel and watching it (just looking actually)with a mind that is captured with thoughts she fails in erasing. And she suddenly noticed the sound of the doorbell.

At first, she thought of changing and going as she was in her pajamas and a t-shirt but then she was wondering - "who will come at this hour to

meet me-must be someone out of work"... She opened the gate with disappointment in her heart and a hopeless face … yes, who is it- and suddenly she is across a face she never could overcome… with a bouquet of red roses… Keith - what are you doing here- she whispered with a choking voice… she almost had tears in eyes but her blank nature

could not portray her emotions that well.

Hi… how are you? How have you been - I… I am really sorry… I couldn't control... I need to talk to you…I know I … Stop- she uttered…

come inside- I am sorry my house is in a mess- I don't really get time to
take care of it too much … please have a seat.
Angie, I need it to talk to you- She was busy gathering her broken emotions in a place so that she doesn't lose her mind by settling the drawing-room in a better place to sit and talk…
Angie…..look at me?? Yes, just a second and she rushed to the washroom - locked the door...facing towards the door… and wondering
… is this for real or am I imagining him again….what is it??? Why is i

t happening now???
Angie are you okay? Yes give me a moment- she came outside in a well-maintained way... Yes, let us go and sit in the drawing-room…
Both sitting where she was sitting alone for ages dreaming of this day …
A table with just one chair- Pull the armchair beside the sofa…..she asked... Yes, he replied - don't you think you should be keeping at least two chairs at your dining table…
Why?? With smudged shoulders - I live alone here and no one really comes here … or rather I live here in isolation …
What is the matter why are you here?
Angie- I am a married man now- with a baby girl who is two and a half
years of age. Her restrained eyes turned towards the bouquet- thank you

for this- (trying to divert what she just heard)... cause it literally broke her heart…

Angie- I am here because even after everything is so perfect in my life -

I am not over you… I search you-your nature-character in everyone I meet- I am not happy with my life –

I feel like committing suicide. ---

What why are you saying all this- is your wife not good or some other issue? tell me maybe I can suggest some good options for you- That's my problem-neither my wife is bad or I have other issues...my life is perfect as it should be- and I want you to search options for "us" not me…. I just know it by now… I can't survive without you... I looked for

you in my wife... My past affairs ...my friends...everyone … it has been

almost 10 years Angie… I can clearly see - you haven't moved on too - I

just want you to know I can only be happy with you….and you can only

be happy with me…. I really don't know who did you date after me- or

maybe I am not sure if you are married or divorced…. I am single- I could never be serious with anyone no matter how hard I tried...she said

looking at him making an intense eye contact…

OH… lucky you-you can't be categorized with people judging what kind

of love is it?? Angie if you say a yes- I will start with the divorce proceedings….

Yes is a very very major thing - I don't even know now how to react to this- I have lived so many years in isolation that I don't really know if I will be able to keep this relation or you happy… I have solely loved you all these while that I don't really think I can express my love the same way… I have longed so much for you these years that I will take ages to trust you again… You might get tired of trying but maybe I will not have any expectations from you…. I have been imagining talking to you for a decade now… how can you expect me to accept this is for real and you won't leave me again??-

I love you… I love you immensely … you are my only love of life- I can't even imagine a day without your thoughts- but that will not change the fact that you left me when I needed you the most… you left me clueless about my mistake-I kept wondering for ages-what went wrong?

It took me a long tiring time to understand that there wasn't actually a single time I have betrayed you or a single time I did anything against you… it took me ages to forgive myself for a mistake I never did…

I respect you are coming to my house- but I need time to rethink about this.

Angie, you can take a decade more- this time my actions will prove my love, not my words which were found fake… I have made the biggest mistake by letting you go and making you suffer till now- I made you this isolated person which you never were- I betrayed your trust… I did everything I shouldn't have….but all I know is that I tried- I tried to be away - I tried to move on- but not a single day has passed when I have slept without thinking of you... I have imagined you too in every female I met… as a friend...as a fling...as anyone… moreover, I imagine you each time I touch my wife. If you have time we shall talk about it someday as to why I had to do what I did…. As of now…. I will give you your breathing space…..take your time...here is my number just text me once you feel you can give me a chance to explain… - hands a small note with name and number at the table- stands up towards the exit door-

After reaching the door- one last thing Angie- you look beautiful. And I have never come across a better person than you… even if you don't give me that chance - give yourself a chance- as anyone would be lucky to have you… it's me who never had the sense...and thank you so much for loving me so much that it is sufficient for a lifetime. Bye...

As soon as the door closes- her long wait of holding emotions outbursts... She just couldn't understand how exactly did this happen- she so badly wanted to hug him that she sat on the chair he was sitting -

and imagined him in a hundred of ways she wanted to. She kissed the note he left so many times... With tears in her eyes rolling down as his number almost smudged.... She quickly added him on her phone and then ... the flashbacks started....

It all starts and ends with love - that's what she had in her mind all the time. It was a cozy winter evening; she had a glass of rose wine in one hand and remote of the television which she wasn't concentrating on. It was almost a habitual thing about her every day when she turned up at her lonely house. Switching on the TV -changing channels and not remembering the content of the last one... then going back to where it started finally ending up on a channel and watching it (just looking actually)with a mind that is captured with thoughts she fails in erasing. And she suddenly noticed the sound of the doorbell.

At first, she thought of changing and going as she was in her pajamas and a t-shirt but then she was wondering - "who will come at this hour to meet me-must be someone out of work"... She opened the gate with disappointment in her heart and a hopeless face ... yes, who is it- and suddenly she is across a face she never could overcome... with a bouquet of red roses... Keith - what are you doing here- she whispered with a choking voice... she almost had tears in eyes but her blank nature could not portray her emotions that well.

Hi... how are you? How have you been - I... I am really sorry... I couldn't control... I need to talk to you...I know I ... Stop- she uttered... come inside- I am sorry my house is in a mess- I don't really get time to take care of it too much … please have a seat.

Angie, I need it to talk to you- She was busy gathering her broken emotions in a place so that she doesn't lose her mind by settling the drawing-room in a better place to sit and talk…

Angie…..look at me?? Yes, just a second and she rushed to the washroom - locked the door...facing towards the door… and wondering

… is this for real or am I imagining him again….what is it???

Why is it happening now??? Angie are you okay? Yes give me a moment- she came outside in a well- maintained way... Yes, let us go and sit in the drawing-room…

Both sitting where she was sitting alone for ages dreaming of this day …

A table with just one chair- Pull the armchair beside the sofa…..she asked... Yes, he replied - don't you think you should be keeping at least two chairs at your dining table…

Why?? With smudged shoulders - I live alone here and no one really comes here … or rather I live here in isolation …

What is the matter why are you here?

Angie- I am a married man now- with a baby girl who is two and a half

years of age. Her restrained eyes turned towards the bouquet- thank you

for this- (trying to divert what she just heard)... cause it literally broke her heart…

Angie- I am here because even after everything is so perfect in my life -

I am not over you… I search you-your nature-character in everyone I meet- I am not happy with my life –

I feel like committing suicide. ---
What why are you saying all this- is your wife not good or some other issue? tell me maybe I can suggest some good options for you- That's my problem-neither my wife is bad or I have other issues...my life is perfect as it should be- and I want you to search options for "us" not me.... I just know it by now... I can't survive without you... I looked for
you in my wife... My past affairs ...my friends...everyone ... it has been almost 10 years Angie... I can clearly see - you haven't moved on too - I
just want you to know I can only be happy with you....and you can only
be happy with me.... I really don't know who did you date after me- or
maybe I am not sure if you are married or divorced.... I am single- I could never be serious with anyone no matter how hard I tried...she said
looking at him making an intense eye contact...
OH... lucky you-you can't be categorized with people judging what kind
of love is it?? Angie if you say a yes- I will start with the divorce proceedings....
Yes is a very very major thing - I don't even know now how to react to this- I have lived so many years in isolation that I don't really know if I will be able to keep this relation or you happy... I have solely loved you
all these while that I don't really think I can express my love the same way... I have longed so much for you these years that I will take ages to

trust you again… You might get tired of trying but maybe I will not have any expectations from you…. I have been imagining talking to you
for a decade now… how can you expect me to accept this is for real and
you won't leave me again??-
I love you… I love you immensely … you are my only love of life- I can't even imagine a day without your thoughts- but that will not change
the fact that you left me when I needed you the most… you left me clueless about my mistake-I kept wondering for ages-what went wrong?
It took me a long tiring time to understand that there wasn't actually a single time I have betrayed you or a single time I did anything against you… it took me ages to forgive myself for a mistake I never did…

I respect you are coming to my house- but I need time to rethink about this.
Angie, you can take a decade more- this time my actions will prove my love, not my words which were found fake… I have made the biggest mistake by letting you go and making you suffer till now- I made you this isolated person which you never were- I betrayed your trust… I did
everything I shouldn't have….but all I know is that I tried- I tried to be
away - I tried to move on- but not a single day has passed when I have slept without thinking of you... I have imagined you too in every female
I met… as a friend...as a fling...as anyone… moreover, I imagine you

each time I touch my wife. If you have time we shall talk about it someday as to why I had to do what I did.... As of now.... I will give you your breathing space.....take your time...here is my number just text

me once you feel you can give me a chance to explain... - hands a small

note with name and number at the table- stands up towards the exit door-

After reaching the door- one last thing Angie- you look beautiful. And I

have never come across a better person than you... even if you don't give me that chance - give yourself a chance- as anyone would be lucky to have you... it's me who never had the sense...and thank you so much

for loving me so much that it is sufficient for a lifetime. Bye...

As soon as the door closes- her long wait of holding emotions outbursts... She just couldn't understand how exactly did this happen- she so badly wanted to hug him that she sat on the chair he was sitting -

and imagined him in a hundred of ways she wanted to. She kissed the note he left so many times... With tears in her eyes rolling down as his number almost smudged.... She quickly added him on her phone and then ... the flashbacks started....

2. FLASHBACKS

Flashbacks- The present and the past coexist, but the past shouldn't be in
flashback. how do you think someone handles flashbacks- clearly she wasn't good at it- it took her a really long time to accept his memories to
be a part of her life- all she ever wanted to do was to live happily in the world full of memories that she created apart from her practical world which she was living in… Isn't it difficult to just start living with the memories?? Isn't it really very hard?? As she was crying herself to sleep-her eyes kept remembering the first time she met him.
It wasn't exactly like love at first sight. It was more like she didn't even notice him the first time she met him. And maybe it didn't matter ...because the connection already started...maybe she didn't feel it by then but maybe he felt it right there and then... One month had passed by- and no communication started… ever since they first met...she had
gone back to her regular life and almost forgot-the short meeting too- On
a drowsy morning after a crazy party...she got up and was scrolling her phone… and there she sees - "100 missed calls" ….. What???? Who is this crazy person who was calling me throughout the night …?
She decides to call back on the number….
Ringing ….
Hello- Hi- who is this may I know I received a crazy amount of missed calls from this number. Hi- it's me

Who??

Keith… OH… hi! But why did you call me so many times?

Why didn't you answer? Where the hell were you?

Excuse me?? No one has ever talked to me like that…

OH- I … I am sorry then …

No not for so that you say sorry -oh god!! Anyway, how have you been?? I am good but ever since you left I have been thinking about you

- I don't know what's over me but all I know is that I want to be friends with you… So will you be my friend??

Ahhh… yes… why not… but just a small thing I don't have habits of interference from anyone … no one has ever shown any kind of rights on me. So it will be great if you will respect this.

Sure- but in my opinion, there are no relations without a few rights on each other….still I will try… His words made her rethink about relationships- with a subtle voice she said Hey listen don't feel bad- we can give it a try just give it a little more time. With a happy voice, he said: sure.

After days and weeks of talking every day for a minimum of 8 hours per day, she discovered that she was developing a habit of him-which she didn't want because of her reserved nature.

The phone rings at night she picks it up - hello-

Hi… (With excitement) did you reach home?

Yes

what happened you sound low??? No …

Yes…

Bunk it...

No say …

Alright if you really want to know….I feel we are getting too close…I am developing a habit of you which I don't want to lose me have fear within me of losing you… I can't be weak…I can't be doing this… what

we talk about how we talk is not like friends anymore…so let's take a break and talk less.

Keith with a breath of relief- Phew! I got scared…

I am serious Keith … don't joke…

Hey hey hey… relax… firstly it's okay to be weak at some times it is human Secondly, who told you I love you in a way a friend loves a friend… I LOVE YOU…. In every way possible way- in every way, it should be… in every way anyone has to love anyone or in every way anyone can imagine to be loved … in every way you see the love in stories… in every way; you see it in movies… I just love you truly - madly - deeply… without any expectations of you loving me or we were

in a relationship. I really want that we do… but even if we don't… I will

love you all my life till I last breathe like this… I will be this possessive and concerned about you forever….I am dying to hear that you love me

too but I know you might never do so….Still, each time you answer my

call at a single ring I feel you will eventually fall for me someday….. I feel like singing and jumping out of excitement each time your number

flashes on my phone screen… I feel like giving a million kisses to my

phone after you hang up…. I keep dreaming about spending time with
you in person every single moment of my day… and even when I am trying to doze off for the day… I keep imagining you beside me …. Hugging me…I don't know if whatever I am sharing with you right now...will have any effect or will you even know how I feel about you…
But I just wanted to shout loud about my feelings towards you…I just want you to know that I am there for you….today- tomorrow and forever
as long as I am alive….I don't just love you … I am crazy about you… so….. I …. I guess I over spoke…. I …. I …. I …. am sorry….if you felt
bad…please don't leave talking to me for this (getting paranoid)...don't block me the way you block everyone who proposed you….I… can't

afford to lose you...I…
Shhhhh- she replied
Silence…..of almost a minute …. I LOVE YOU TOO….. That was it…. The starting towards the love of a lifetime.

Flashbacks- The present and the past coexist, but the past shouldn't be in
flashback. how do you think someone handles flashbacks- clearly she wasn't good at it- it took her a really long time to accept his memories to
be a part of her life- all she ever wanted to do was to live happily in the world full of memories that she created apart from her practical world which she was living in… Isn't it difficult to just start living with

the memories?? Isn't it really very hard?? As she was crying herself to sleep-her eyes kept remembering the first time she met him.
It wasn't exactly like love at first sight. It was more like she didn't even notice him the first time she met him. And maybe it didn't matter ...because the connection already started...maybe she didn't feel it by then but maybe he felt it right there and then... One month had passed by- and no communication started… ever since they first met...she had
gone back to her regular life and almost forgot-the short meeting too- On
a drowsy morning after a crazy party...she got up and was scrolling her phone… and there she sees - "100 missed calls" ….. What???? Who is this crazy person who was calling me throughout the night …?
She decides to call back on the number….
Ringing ….
Hello- Hi- who is this may I know I received a crazy amount of missed calls from this number. Hi- it's me
Who??
Keith… OH… hi! But why did you call me so many times?
Why didn't you answer? Where the hell were you?
Excuse me?? No one has ever talked to me like that…
OH- I … I am sorry then …

No not for so that you say sorry -oh god!! Anyway, how have you been?? I am good but ever since you left I have been thinking about you
- I don't know what's over me but all I know is that I want to be friends with you… So will you be my friend??
Ahhh… yes… why not… but just a small thing I don't have habits of

interference from anyone … no one has ever shown any kind of rights on me. So it will be great if you will respect this.

Sure- but in my opinion, there are no relations without a few rights on each other….still I will try… His words made her rethink about relationships- with a subtle voice she said Hey listen don't feel bad- we can give it a try just give it a little more time. With a happy voice, he said: sure.

After days and weeks of talking every day for a minimum of 8 hours per day, she discovered that she was developing a habit of him-which she didn't want because of her reserved nature.

The phone rings at night she picks it up - hello-

Hi… (With excitement) did you reach home?

Yes

what happened you sound low??? No …

Yes…

Bunk it...

No say …

Alright if you really want to know….I feel we are getting too close…I am developing a habit of you which I don't want to lose me have fear within me of losing you… I can't be weak…I can't be doing this… what

we talk about how we talk is not like friends anymore…so let's take a break and talk less.

Keith with a breath of relief- Phew! I got scared…

I am serious Keith … don't joke…

Hey hey hey… relax… firstly it's okay to be weak at some times it is human Secondly, who told you I love you in a way a friend loves a friend… I LOVE YOU…. In every way possible way- in every way, it

should be… in every way anyone has to love anyone or in every way anyone can imagine to be loved … in every way you see the love in stories… in every way; you see it in movies… I just love you truly - madly - deeply… without any expectations of you loving me or we were
in a relationship. I really want that we do… but even if we don't… I will
love you all my life till I last breathe like this… I will be this possessive and concerned about you forever….I am dying to hear that you love me
too but I know you might never do so….Still, each time you answer my
call at a single ring I feel you will eventually fall for me someday….. I feel like singing and jumping out of excitement each time your number
flashes on my phone screen… I feel like giving a million kisses to my phone after you hang up…. I keep dreaming about spending time with
you in person every single moment of my day… and even when I am trying to doze off for the day… I keep imagining you beside me …. Hugging me…I don't know if whatever I am sharing with you right now...will have any effect or will you even know how I feel about you…
But I just wanted to shout loud about my feelings towards you…I just want you to know that I am there for you….today- tomorrow and forever
as long as I am alive….I don't just love you … I am crazy about you… so….. I …. I guess I over spoke…. I …. I …. I …. am sorry….if you felt

bad…please don't leave talking to me for this (getting paranoid)...don't block me the way you block everyone who proposed you….
I… can't afford to lose you...I… Shhhhh- she replied
Silence…..of almost a minute …. I LOVE YOU TOO….. That was it…. The starting towards the love of a lifetime.

3. LOVE IS UNCONTROLLABLE

Love is a crazy feeling… you feel the person you love even if they are not around… That was exactly how it started Angie started feeling Keith's presence
everywhere around her….Before she could realize anything, it turned into an obsession of seeing Keith talking to him…
You know it all seemed like a movie scene in real life … except the part that in movies the character is fictional representing their characters and
it ends in a few hours; whereas here it was happening in real… moreover, it seemed never-ending and this obsession of imagining Keith
around her was taking over her sanity at a slow steady pace…
Angie was jobless that time when it all happened, she was looking for a
decent position according to her profile…sitting at her sofa set she remembers why she did quit her previous job the time when Keith had called her up and said "I am sorry Angie but we can't be together, I have
started feeling we are not meant to be a couple, you are not the one for me, and somehow I have started to dislike you being around me" … this
moment and words changed everything for Angie… she quit her dream
job … spent each day at house arrest, sentenced herself to this

punishment without being at fault; she kept wondering as to where did
she lack ??? What was it that she couldn't give Keith- for him to think that he doesn't like being around her anymore…
Gradually these few days of a breakup mode happen in everyone's life … isn't it? The time you hopelessly try to get over someone … the time you wonder how and why did it all start when it had to end this way… the time when all you have in mind is a fear of doubt if you can move on
or will it give you a series of disappointments…. The time when most of
us are in serious, depressed moods when our friends are trying to cheer us up… when over partying, drinking is a way you think you can forget

your partner …I guess we all have gone through this, dealt with it in our
own respective ways…
In Angie's case, she had a hard time saying things about how it is… she
was always like the strong one in the group… she always had a smile on
her face whereas her inner self seems dead to her… the moment Keith had asked her to go away from his life all she had was a blank mind, a blank soul and a blank behavior… Keith was everything to her … all her
emotions, feelings, desires were just equaled to Keith being in her life loving her, being around her… she was broken from within something

which we call not repairable ... she spent months in just one position on
her couch staring at the TV with no idea what's going on... until one day she saw him ...(imagination)... somehow she knew it was her imagination that she is seeing him but the cravings for seeing him were more than the acceptance power that all of this is imaginary... and right
from that moment till the doorbell Keith was actually never gone... he was there ... so much around here that the real Keith coming at her doorstep came as a reality check which Angie was not ready to face... That is the thing about pain ... it can only be understood by the one who
has gone through it deeply, for everyone else no matter how much they love you its something you can control and tame... but in reality, can someone do it? no – it is a highly uncontrollable feeling... love is an uncontrollable emotion... Love makes you fall weak at knees and yet powerful at heart... love is the only pain that affects mentally but hurts physically as well... you actually feel your heart breaking into pieces ...
and so was happening with Angie... the stranger at the door scared her ... not because it all will start again or she will be heartbroken again but
the fact that her imaginary Keith will disappear ... All these years have made Angie addicted to the obsession of Keith – she had his shirts stored
in a zipper so that it doesn't lose its fragrance ...which eventually was

lost with time... his letters and cards were something that Angie had preserved ...her life was all about Keith ... Keith...Keith... how can

someone love so madly…deeply…
It has been ages since he had left but Angie is all about Keith… after months of house arrest she finally did come out and had joined a new office someplace she did not like … and that day after she had returned from office to her usual routine drills when Keith was at the doorstep and she was back to blank…
Love is complicated just like the emotions and graphs of Angie's personality…love can make you want someone as badly you ever wanted and also hate them at the same time for treating you bad… love
will make you beg them for attention and also fight with them for unwanted reasons… love can make you sacrifice things for the one you love but also make you want them more than ever….
And there it goes mixed emotions of flashbacks and reality … clashes in her mind as if initiating a war she wasn't ready to fight…

4. LOVE IS THE RISK

Have you ever traveled on a train??? it's a beautiful feeling….Especially because of the hours of the journey it just unwittingly urges you to think… about everything you don't get the time
to think with the busy lifestyle we humans have to maintain….you know the only thing that keeps flashing in Angie's mind….is the moment Keith had proposed her for the first time...it flashes like … a dream ...she had almost forgotten how he feels for real….she had been without him so much that she doesn't want to be away from the beautiful feeling she gets in dreaming about him…. Imagining him The first time he had ever touch her … was the day she realized how immensely incomplete she was till then…. And she almost had Goosebumps thinking about it…. The touch ….. It was like something...that's not physical… it was like someone touched her soul...for the very first time… She stopped herself from thinking …. Immediately … and just reminded herself- he is your disease you have been struggling to survive-taking medicines for almost forever ... lost all
contact with the outer world...proved your family you are mentally unstable…. Now, why… She doesn't have the answer to this- all she is aware of….is that Keith is the only one that can make or break her… she
has almost become unaffected to every other person she knows….. You know one should judge love by the number of beautiful memories it

has created not the part that maybe just got you under the pressure of not
loving someone because you can't make them unloved.
Angie had suffered a lot in the past years… she had lost her sanity to her
love… she had been under psychiatric supervision for the imaginations she had … and she has forgotten the difference between imagination and
reality… and with so much to cope up with and match the requirements

of daily life…she had almost given up on trying to rebuild her life- although it's the most essential thing to do… but unlike any other normal human being- she is too strong as a woman and too weak as a human… she is ready to start living her life but not ready to accept Keith
is never coming back… she is okay in moving on… but not without him
or his memories...she is ready for the world but not ready to compromise
on her imaginary world…. And in between of all these self-preparation for years….she gets to see him…. All of a sudden at her doorsteps…. It's
too much to handle at once … and more than that it's too hard for Angie with all the imaginations she is living with ….. All of a sudden …. Seeing him… she had almost lost her sanity…. She wants him not to
leave ever again… but she definitely can't say this…. She wants to hug

him and cry but she is too strong now to do that....She wants to slap him

and ask where was he the whole time...but she is too reserved to do that....she wants to kiss him madly but she is too worried to do that....

Angie has changed a lot in the past years not as in characteristics or nature....But she has gone too quiet to be handled by anyone.... She doesn't complain if she is hurt... she is okay with canceled plans... she is more than happy to stay alone....She is the calmest person to talk about irritating issues.... She doesn't care if someone is ethically wrong towards her...she is carrying different personalities with different environments.... Keith at her door has made her mind agitate to the utmost limit....but holding on everything aside with her one undying desire of being with him –

She picks up her phone and calls him-- The phone rings and her heart pounding to a heart rate of 200 ...plus.... He answers the phone - thank

god you called I was dying in the thoughts that would you call me or I have failed the attempt.

How can you fail the attempt?-

I failed in my attempts of being away, so now what??

Keith- can we meet?

Angie- where?

Keith- at your place? Tonight for dinner?

Angie- Alright...At 8 PM.

Keith - can't wait to see you....

Angie- (ignoring what he said in spite of wanting to answer badly) what will you have?

Keith- Chinese? I will get it from our favorite restaurant with wine? Is it

okay?

Angie- it's not the first date- why all this??

Keith- maybe to a fresh start…

Angie- we have not mutually agreed to that yet…

Keith- yes I know I was just …. Still Chinese and wine make a romantic

couple...will get it...

Angie- ha-ha...alright… see you.

5. I AM ALL ABOUT YOU

"SEE YOU – for dinner " I have been seeing him for dinner for ages... how on earth am I going to handle my emotions in front of him, what will happen next... has he come back in my life to have fun with me and

leave again ...

These thoughts were making Angie nervous for the dinner ... the thought that she did say yes to Keith but the feelings of again getting betrayed by him were making her anxious...

No matter how bad you want someone back the feeling of them leaving

you always have greater power over your mind.... You can love someone a lot to get your heart broken by them again but the mind always lets you know that your heart can maybe love and love with grace ... take the pain of separation with grace but your mind will be messed up... life will not be the same anymore... regular routines will not be the same anymore... you will not be the same anymore...

But in the fight between heart and mind... the heart always wins with major points....

Points remain as simple as but I love him/her...

Angie loved Keith and there was nothing beyond that she questioned...

she knew that maybe Keith has come back with a motive or maybe just to have fun with her again... but she couldn't help it she could not help

falling for him in every glimpse of him at his very look at the door at his
every word and tone of voice… she was in love with him and there was nothing more than that she could understand … it hurts to be around him
knowing he is married but all she cared about was he is with him at this
moment … all hers for as long as he will be there for dinner…
Chinese and wine … he still remembers what can melt Angie …
Angie just couldn't let go of the opportunity she was about to get to see
him in real and be with him maybe if it would just last for this dinner …
maybe nothing can be right with them but he seems right to her… in every way…
As Angie settles her mind for dinner … making her heart calm down a
bit by listening to music… the time is here … its dinner time … its Keith
and my alone time … It's just about how much and how deeply I love him…. Maybe it's just a dinner and I am over hyper… but I can't help the butterflies in my stomach…
I just hope it starts and never ends…
I love you, Keith – she smiled seeing herself in the mirror…imagining she is saying it to Keith

6. NERVOUSNESS

You talk more when you are nervous- isn't it? What is making you nervous Angie?? Is it me?? Or the time gap we have gone through…

None of it Keith - stop acting as if you know me?

Angie if you aren't ready to forgive me … it's okay… but don't judge my
love for you.

Love can be seen in actions Keith- if you really did love me all of this or
nothing of this would have happened…

I know Angie- I have ruined everything between us- and moreover for you…. But little do you know about that along with you I destroyed my
own self too- I got away from you and I suffered ...you at least could blame me… I was cursing myself throughout … and all of these for what??? Misunderstandings….?? I am a human Angie- I fell for this shit
… I fell for this that you don't love me… and moreover, in that period of
a dilemma, I had to forcibly get married… and I know I could have disagreed and fought… but all I wanted that moment was to get away from you… and I chose the wrong option … I suffered too Angie… I died too… I was lost too… I cried too…

But no matter in regards to your pain my pain is much lesser… I lived my life and realized it much later… that I can't live without you whereas

you were just mine all this time- you knew that you love me only me- and can't live without me… I was suffering throughout with the thoughts
that would you be hating me now?? Are you in love with someone else the same way?? Is someone touching you the way I do?? I was burning in hell all the time Angie-
At least you know what you want - how you want - you had the freedom
of emotions…. I was forced to make decisions… forced to feel emotions
I don't want to feel...forced in a relationship I was hating all the while...I
thought of giving my marriage a try... But what I did to you she did to me … Cheating behind my back…. And I was still forced to be with her...sleep with her...keep her happy… I was used by my family ...for a stature, I could have never been able to handle...Now tell me, Angie was

I really happy all these times? Yes you are right I realized it really late that you were, are and will always be my only love…. I let you suffer alone, become something you weren't … isolated you completely from this world and even worse I am your disease...that too an incurable one… I am solely responsible for every miss-happening in your life… I
am your culprit….
Stop saying all this Keith there is nothing called your pain and my pain -
that is the point it took me years to explain but unable to make you

understand.... What brought you here Keith...? Why didn't I think about
my already broken heart before calling you here again- why were you and I unable to move on in our respective lives????
It's because- it's not You and I, it is WE, US ...
We couldn't separate each other from our souls... it is no more a human
connection it's our souls that unite us...I am done ... explaining that... and I am tired of this pretentious way of living.... Look, Keith....
Moving close to him- I don't know about forgiveness and big talks am too small a person to be able to forgive anyone... I just know am not strong enough to lose you again... neither am I prepared for your indecisive nature.... You have to mature sometime in life ... you have to
understand you can't be doing this to me repeatedly...to be really honest
right now at this stage of my life I don't even have the desire that you be
with me as a couple... I have already adjusted with my imaginations....
So if you have no intention of keeping your words ... let this meeting be
our last...
Angie- I could have never imagined that you would be saying this to me... but regardless of that ... I have not been loyal enough for your trust so just spend 2 weeks with me ... if you think I am changed ...give
me a chance ...otherwise, just kick me out .... And let the suffering be mine this time....

Lol… do you think Keith suffering will be only yours…. Just a glimpse of you has deeper effects on me then the medicines I am taking to keep myself normal...so 2 weeks is going to be another step for self-destruction… but I really don't want to be unfair to you… therefore let

us do this together…. And leave rest on destiny…..

Let us stop this conversation right here-leave the past where it resides and "try" to make it work… as we both are aware of the fact that we are

nothing without each other …. Absolute destruction ….

Angie can you bless me with a hug- it seems like I have been craving for

it since the time I was born...ever since you left life seems unmanageable….

Keith - come closer…

"Finally the hug'

Angie…..

Shhhhhh….don't say anything …. Let me hear your heart beat….

Let me have your fragrance on me….

"The only thing Angie's heart and mind were screaming within was … I

LOVE YOU KEITH-I LOVE YOU MADLY…. I HAVE BEEN DREAMING ABOUT THIS FOR A LIFETIME …. I AM ALL YOURS … ALWAYS HAVE BEEN AND ALWAYS WILL REMAIN…"

7. SOME LOVE CRAVINGS

The hug continued for almost 15 minutes… without a single word spoken by both of them … and then out of sudden reaction, Keith utters-

I have a surprise for you, Angie…. Would you like to …..

Surprise …. What is it says Angie (with excitement)...

Can we step out of the house???

I am not dressed up for going out Keith …can I dress up …

No need Angie ...you look pretty even without dressing up and we are not going any place where you would be uncomfortable with you are wearing ….

Angie (in doubt) alright ….

As soon as she steps out she sees a beautiful decoration arrangement right outside her house … Two chairs and a table in white with a red table mat right in the middle of the small garden she used to love spending time at … a bottle of champagne with 2 glasses with their names engraved on it… a cake that says thank you for loving me so much… A greeting card that says for the most beautiful girl in the world…. A bunch of roses rightly made into a beautiful bouquet…. A handwritten note that says - I would never want anything more from life

except a destiny that lets me be with you all my life…

Keith pulls the chair for Angie – be seated, princess

Angie is overwhelmed with this arrangement - she never even imagined that all of these can ever happen again ...sitting with butterflies in her stomach and a pounding heart…

He pulls a chair for himself and sits right opposite her facing her directly.

Let's cut the cake first???

Hands over the beautifully crafted knife covered with red and black ribbon to Angie …

Angie makes a wish…..and cut the cake …..

Angie closes her eyes - and wishes that this moment of immense happiness that she is getting shouldn't be destroyed by anything …..opens her eyes with tears filled but not rolling down …

Cuts the cake...removes a slice and moved her hand towards Keith's mouth….

Then Keith picks up a slice and makes her eat.

The cake was from Honeywell bakery Angie's favorite bakery …

Is the cake the dinner for us tonight asked Angie with a smirk.

No just wait and watch -

Suddenly a waiter arrives all dressed up with a chef's cap stating at the service of ms.angie…

How romantic Keith….Angie whispers….

What would you like to eat ?? questions the waiter

Ahhhhh - how is it possible to get whatever I want to eat right now with

no restaurants nearby and no kitchen equipment???

Just command me your wish mam… it's my duty to present to you what

you like….

(Keith was staring her continuously from the start…)

Mmmm I would like to have Hakka noodles and veg Manchurian with
gravy….
Keith started laughing out loud suddenly…
What's wrong with you why are you laughing? Simultaneously the waiter passed a smile…
Mam sir already ordered the same and its kept inside….I will just get it…..
Angie- you still are the same…. I knew you will order this ….
Keith, You still remember I like Chinese food when eating out ??
I remember everything Angie- because not for a single moment were you out of my heart and mind….
I...I don't know what to say...to you Keith….
Then let us start our dinner….
Unending conversations- even after dinner was long over and deserts were completed …
It is cold here Angie- let's go inside the house…
Holding hands and moving towards the house…. As soon as they enter the house gate and it shuts …. The long urge of a physical desire… just
came over them… Keith covers Angie's waist with his left hand… with a forceful gesture of pulling her closer to him….
Angie's heart rate was already touching its limits….
They look at each other with intensity…. Followed by a passionate long
kiss …. That lasted more than the 5-minute hug….
Keith slowly placed his lips on her neck….the more he touched her the

more she felt like surrendering herself to him....she was so much under
the spell of his fragrance that she almost gave up on her every condition
she made to herself before giving him a last chance....
Indulging in the kiss they move towards the bedroom... not for a single
moment did they leave each other....before entering the room.... Finally
landing on Angie's bed where she cried almost every night for him ....
Undressing each other passionately they made love to each other in a way as if they were dying every day of their lives without each other... the cravings the thirst for each other brought them a little closer that night ....
It was 4 AM - Angie got up covering her bare body with the blanket and
moving towards the washroom... after she moves out of the washroom -
she sits right beside Keith- looking at him with all the love she cannot show him when is awake.... And all of a sudden she recalls every moment of sorrow she had gone through- every time she went to her counselor and spoke only about him- every time she took a pill to sleep-
and every time she took a pill to handle her anxiety attacks... every time
she was prescribed with anxiety calming injection...which was too painful in the starting days.... And how slowly each physical pain was way lesser than the mental pain she was going through.....7 years of life

without him- 7 years of separation and 7 years of psychological disorders she went through....

I made love to him again... why am I doing this to myself...? What if he

betrays me again... what if he vanishes like a dream that doesn't happen

twice.... Too many thoughts came over her...and she sat on the couch holding her pillow...and thinking ....what is it that she falls weak in front

of him... why she desires only him ....

It was 9 AM then- when Keith woke up....

You didn't sleep Angie- he said rubbing his eyes....

I did...

Got up at 4 ....

What are doing since then??

I was thinking about why we did what we did last night ....

Angie doesn't regret it at least- it was my happiest night after we got separated...

And I thought you were happy too but...........

I am happy Keith but I am scared to even more extent... I won't be able

to stand any more heartbreak....I won't be able to survive after it....

Nothing will happen Angie ... trust me!!!

8. TRUST ME OR TRUST ME NOT

"TRUST ME" – how is it possible after years of thinking he never really
loved her- how is it possible after dozens of sleepless nights – how is it possible after reaching at the edge of death every night feeling suicidal … how is it possible after losing her mind over him, after forcefully taking pills to stop seeing him but skipping it so that she does….
"Trust me"- was a big thing for Angie
As flashbacks run in her mind it takes her to the day when they were separated … Angie had called him from different numbers, begged him
to take her back, cried in front of him a million times, stalked him to see
him once and drugged herself with pills so much that she never really has to be in senses to think about him….
That's how bad loving someone hurts especially when they no longer feel the same for you… in my opinion love can only happen and you cannot undo it…. Love means just loving someone unconditionally forever… you can never hate someone you love… you might dislike them for some reason… but hate is a very strong emotion and people who have love in their hearts can never really hate anyone…
That's exactly what Angie could never do even when Keith left her out of no major reason, she could never really hate him, she always had his good memories stored inside her mind and heart… but the worst part

about trust is once it's broken it can never be the same… you can be hurt by a person and forgive them a million times but trusting them again is something our minds never agree to… our hearts love them so much that we end up forgiving them but our minds have a hard time trusting them that they won't do it again…

Angie loves Keith a lot… more than she could ever love herself… selflessly, unconditionally, deeply and just too madly … Keith the name itself was a name to which her heart skips a beat… to which her

emotions rejoice to…. But trusting him again on things he has messed up in the past is something Angie was afraid of doing...

Love has the power to turn fear into positivity … and Angie's love for Keith was beyond her fears… she decided in her mind that if a trust is what my destiny with Keith requires I will do it again… if I am supposed to be broken again I will… if I do not have Keith in my destiny I will lose him again but at least I will be knowing it deep inside me that I tried till the last chance…

For Keith, every chance matters, for him every breath …and for his love every risk … my heart is open to, my mind is helpless to and my soul is hungry to… because Keith is all I have and Keith will always be everything I will ever want…I love him madly…

Snapping back to the conversation Angie looked at Keith hugged him and -

9. WORTH THE RISK

"Trust me" always had a bad experience for Angie- but on the verge of losing him again made her terrified soul say - okay, Keith, I Trust You !!

Although their souls were destined to be together but physically together

was a big step…

Angie quickly made breakfast –so that they can both leave for work together ….

But as soon as Keith stepped out of the room he was all ready to leave

He looked at Angie and the table she prepared for breakfast

Both of them still too much in love with last night looking at each other

while they finish their breakfast together …

Keith gets up and utters in a stammering voice – I have to go to my house …

Before he could complete the sentence Angie gets up and says it's okay- leave …

Angie I...

It's okay Keith don't give explanations you owe it to your wife as well. I

understand (with a fake smile)

Thank God! I thought you would be pissed

Ha-ha Angie smirked ... No, I am not pissed- There is a difference between pissed and hurt …

What do you mean – Keith questioned

Nothing- we both are running late, let us leave...

Well, can I drop you somewhere?

No, I booked a cab … thanks anyway

Keith had this in his mind that Angie wasn't okay but he was aware that

she won't let him touch her wounds too …with regret of letting Angie go in a cab he sits in his car and starts off for his house …

As soon as he arrives his daughter jumps on him with joy and as soon as

he hugs her he suffers from a guilt ride thinking about her future …

What am I doing? Just because you can't survive without Angie and that

she is the solo happiness you have, you can't ruin the life of your child- it's not her fault if you could never love her mother –

Maybe its karma – that even after Angie has agreed to be with you again

maybe you are not right for her this time…maybe you will hurt her more

this time so before it's too late talk to Angie and leave her so that she is not a part of your miserable life and suffer. She forgives you at once without thinking anything and again you will bring her back to the dark

state…

But what about the promises I made her last night – it was not fake it was out of love (Keith is talking to himself in his mind he is losing control)

Suddenly Githa (Keith's daughter) her name was a combination name of Keith and Angie which he kept at the time of her birth…

Screams- papa …

(Keith is suffering from brokenness at this moment)

Yes, kiddo tell me?

Where were you papa mom got worried?

At office princess, papa had lots of pending work

He hands over Githa over to Dinah (his wife) and enters his room after locking his door He kneels down on the floor with all his broken pieces thinking what should he do now Neither can I live without Angie nor can I let Githa suffer a punishment she doesn't deserve…

Keith somehow gathers his courage and move towards the bathroom …to get ready for office.

As he was leaving for the office he picks up Githa kisses her and leaves for office.

As he sat in his car he promises himself – whoever I think more about after being busy at the office will be my decision and destiny for life… no looking anywhere else after I made the decision… And if by any chance it is not Angie I will not take those 13 days from us no matter what… I would make the most of those days and give Angie all the love

I have in me for her.

And if by any chance its Githa I will take her and Dinah for a holiday and arrange everything for her bright future on her mother's name so that they don't have to suffer financially at least. Wow, how impossible is it for me to be happy I lose at both ends – Sighs!

Suddenly his phone rings it's a text from Angie saying – **would you be coming home today as well?** (Keith can't help blushing at her text) but

too much mind work is happening for him so he replied

Not sure will let you know in a while –how is your day going at work?

He was continuously waiting for her reply back to this but no message received

Meanwhile – As soon as Angie sat in the cab she kept thinking –(the same time Keith was thinking on his way home and at home)

You are doing it again ? you are again going to ruin yourself and the poor kid of Keith who is not at all at fault in this whole scenario. Just because you are greedy for him and his love you will break his family …

really? this is not you Angie …. Weren't you surviving before he came that day … Cant, you love him like this forever, it is not important to get

who you love – loving them truly is important- you can't really do this to

that kid. Just think all this time you were in the middle of nowhere thinking has Keith ever loved you truly or was it just a phase but now you are sure he loved you he still does and maybe he always will .. Isn't it enough for survival … suddenly tears roll down her eyes uncontrollably after realizing that maybe she won't be around again and

the emptiness will be back in a more dangerous way.

She promises himself that she won't meet Keith after 13 days and she will shift her home to some different city that Keith would never find out

(remember Keith made a promise to himself at the same time).

No matter what we deserve these 13 days… I will love him beyond doubts … beyond the word love itself…just when she realizes 13 days is

too less a time for enough love to be captured for her soul... she picks her phone and texts him-

Would you be coming home today as well?

Keith's reply made her rethink but all she craves is to spend time with him as much as she can…

So she decided she will text him again by evening to check if he can make it at her house tonight.

10. PATIENCE

A person can have patience in everything in the world… And just how Angie is she was the calmest person as per what life had taught her… but when it turned to patience in love Angie was losing her calm… she was so restless at work that she was unable to sit in her chair for long and had to use the excuse for washroom and phone calls…every half an
hour…

She was inattentive and distant from her work… several times she made
mistakes and was trying really hard to be attentive but all that was running her mind was …what will happen? Will Keith reappear at home?

You know that desirous feeling of loving someone and craving for their presence it's magical and annoying at the same time because your emotions are inexorable … and while restraining yourself you tend to lose the fight to your heart…

Angie was curious to know what was running in Keith's mind and to see
if her destiny allows him to return home again…

Wait and some more wait… Angie was anxious… losing her mind …all
at the same time… but she had to maintain her social behavior somehow…

As the clock ticked 4 PM – Angie was having a small break at her office so she decided to step out of her office for a walk… she bought her

favorite aerated drink from a shop nearby and started to walk towards a
sitting area nearby… as she had a sip of her drink and headphones plugged in with her current favorite song … she just didn't hear a single
word all her mind was filled with thoughts of Keith and an inquisitive nature… she unlocks her phone to check if there are any messages from
Keith but seeing no notifications her heart was sinking …
Well, love is magical… I have learned from movies, stories, and sayings … true passion is not when you are physical with someone's true passion
is when you are intimate with their soul…
With this thought, Angie got up and started walking back to her office it
was exactly 4:45 PM… as she entered there was a power out at her office
everyone was asked to leave … so she decided to get few things for
Keith and prepare for a good night without knowing if he will turn up or
not but her heart was repeatedly saying "maybe he will"…

11. FINALLY, it is YOU

Its almost 7 PM, the day is about to end… it was a really heartbreaking and tough day for Keith and Angie…. It was as if just a day before they felt happiness and a day ahead they have to go back to their respective emptiness….have you ever read an incomplete story?? it's somewhat like that no matter how desperately you want to reach its climax it all depends on the author of the story….in their case maybe the author was
destiny - and it surely never worked in their favor ever… the question is
… why can't two individuals who are incomplete and a disaster without
each other live together… why are they caged separately to suffer till death….
Is it a curse to find your soul mate and be deeply in love with someone? Is it a punishable offense?? I don't really know what is it about except the part that it is the most painful thing in the world… to survive a heartbreak takes courage … but to survive a soul-break is like cutting yourself repeatedly with a dragger and touching the wound million times
in a day…you know it's only going to cause you pain- but there aren't any survival strategies for escape …
Love can give you incredible ways of happiness but as soon as those remembering flashes leave - you find yourself emptier than before … no
doubts about it that sometimes even if you spend a few days with

someone - the memories of it seem to beat with each heartbeat of yours…. There is no better fragrance in the world than the scent of the one you love…. You can move on in life even after someone leaves but the heart and soul that's attached can never really move on- as no matter
how many get together's you attend no one will attract your eyes… No matter how many movies you watch you will relate it …. No matter how
hard you try to get into a relationship...you will end up with comparisons
… that's the irony of love- even after knowing how perfect someone was
for you … you can't be with them neither can you settle for anyone below or above them…sometimes you can try to move ahead in life but
sometimes your heart is stuck to a place you can never travel to….
Keith was preparing his bag to leave the office for the day - and suddenly he recalled the promise he made to himself - and then he tries
to recollect who occupied his mind the whole day… and he notices it was Angie all the time - it was her- he was worried about Githa but…. All he desires and requires is Angie…. He decided that on the 13th day he will propose Angie for marriage…with a request to keep Githa with him… and meanwhile, he will talk about this to Dinah about this - he was more sure about this because he has always noticed that Dinah was not as happy as she seemed and they never really had a bond… it was more than a forceful arrangement their families made and they followed… he decided to talk to Dinah about how she feels about the relationship and then he will disclose Angie to her… for all this, he

planned that he will leave for his house on the 10th day and take them for a vacation for 2 days and there he will take this conversation forward

… with over excitement and butterflies within his pounding heart…. He

picks up his phone and text Angie…" **I am coming"**

Angie was about to leave for the day - when she receives Keith's text

…(she was about to message him after moving out of office premises)…

she blushes… and decides to pick his favorite flowers and wine for the night...with a movie DVD to make the night more interesting…

She picks everything on the way…. And quickly enters the home to make the arrangements … she decides to wear the blue dress he gifted her on their first anniversary...

Keith on the other side calls at his house to inform-

I am traveling for work purposes will be back after a couple of days be ready by then have planned a trip with you and Githa...for 2 days- I have

some serious discussions to make and also I want to spend time with you

both…

Whatever you want -she replied and have a safe trip!!

Thank you - and you too take care and if you need anything in the meantime you can call me…

Alright!! Bye…

Bye….

He dials Angie's number but she doesn't answer - Ahhh!!- I so want to hear her he whispered to himself!!

After 15 minutes he reaches Angie's house … he rings the bell with excitement and happiness about the decision he finally made …. Angie opens the door -

Gosh!!! She is looking so damn pretty in this outfit … she still fits well in it… Keith utters in his mind ….

Angie, you look gorgeous!! Stunning … my mouth is touching the ground….

She blushes and whisper-thank you it's all for you!!

Hugs her immediately … on the door itself…. The door closes on its own...while the hug continued….unconsciously Keith kissed Angie on her neck and say- I love You Angie and there is no greater love than this… I Love you too Keith - I planned a tiny date for you… since its cold outside… let us sit near the fireplace …

Angie Holds his hands and takes him near the fireplace - it was beautifully done… a black colored mattress with maroon bedsheet - two

wine glasses … a bottle of wine … popcorn which she just prepared ….

TV screen placed right opposite to the sitting arrangement with a movie

DVD - and flowers right beside his side of the sitting place….

Wow, Angie!! the arrangement is beautiful just like the love you have for me is….

Let us start the night on this note Angie- we are two inseparable souls…

and we shall always be the same one… by the way… I called you sometime back but I guess you must be busy with the arrangements …. I

am with you here till the 10th day… and post that I have some important

commitment that needs to be sorted … but once I am back from it you
will always find me close enough….
For a moment Angie was too happy about this but as soon as she recalls
her promise to herself she utters why on the 10th day … why not the 13th….
Because it's something very important … and it will change our lives forever….
Angie excuses herself to go washroom- as soon as she enters …. I just had these 13 days with me out of which 3 days are gone…. How am I supposed to react …. What is more, important that this to him?? He is
unaware that I won't ever see him after the 13th day….
Chuck it!! Make the most of what you have got … and leave the rest on
hope…
Washes her face and returns ….
They start the night by raising a toast to their love and switching on the
TV for a movie date night…..

12. INTIMACY IS A SOUL THING

Movie time at home with two lovers is never "just" a movie night ... Keith had his arms around Angie and she was snuggling on his chest ...

his heartbeat was the music she wanted to hear... his compassionate way

of cuddling her was making her weak on her knees... as she placed a kiss on his chest Keith looked at her intensely ... They exchanged looks

that lead to they were so close that their lips almost met... suddenly there was a song in the movie and the volume of the TV got high... Angie moved a bit far from Keith and started to concentrate on the movie...

They both were staring at the screen but none of them were actually concentrating on what was happening in the movie... Keith placed his hand softly on Angie's ... Angie could not resist this at this point she moved towards him and hugged him ... slowly reaching his neck... she

pulled his t-shirt that forced him to come closer to her... as she started to

kiss his neck... moving down to his collar bone she kept kissing him intensely without a pause... Keith was losing his hold on himself he asked Angie to see him – "look at me Angie"... as Angie looked at him he placed his hands to hold Angie's face and moved her hair

backward… placed his lips on Angie's and murmured I LOVE YOU as
he said this his upper and lower lip were co-coordinating with Angie's…
This is what I talk about intimacy… your soul should be filled with love… and intensity … after about 40-45 minutes of loving each other … as soon as Keith got up to use the washroom and returned Angie was
asleep….
She has never had this peaceful sleep WITHOUT her medication in ages…. Keith looked at her smiled and whispered … wow… she looks amazing even while sleeping… I have never come across a person who is so innocent like her… if someone else would have been her ….
she would have never allowed me in her house or life so easily or maybe never allowed… but Angie has the purest heart on this planet more than
herself she loves me and that is exactly what makes me go crazier for her…. I don't know how things will take place the rest of the days but all I know for now is I will fight for her…. I want her to sleep this peacefully every night…. I never want to make her suffer whatever she was suffering… I want to make her happy again… make her full of life again….. Make her smile like before… only a person who loves someone so deeply can forgive a person like me….
Love really has some serious connections…. She was all mine all these years… she proved her loyalty… and me being with my wife could never be her husband…. My soul belongs to Angie since the time we met till the existence of my soul…. I love her…
Thank you so much, God, for showering your blessings on me with the

name- ANGIE....

13. VACATION

Ahhh!!! There is no better happiness in the world than watching her sleep said, Keith –

He covered her with the blanket and removed all the unwanted things from the bed… he picked up the wine bottle …and sat on the couch beside the sleeping arrangement Angie made for him… as he sips the wine he stares at Angie and starts talking to her...

You know you are the only ray of home; you are my sole source of happiness...

My heart beats faster each time I think about you...

I just hope we stay forever this way … I will leave everything and everyone to be with you

I just can't wait to hear the yes from you after I propose you for marriage

Suddenly Angie moves …Keith keeps the wine away moves beside her hugs her and sleeps

The next morning had an incomparable smile on their faces … as if the

hunger of soul love was touched to its peak...

You don't want to go to work? Aren't you going to freshen up? Asked Angie

No, I have taken leave for a few days

What? Why?

To spend time with you and be at your service my highness

Angie blushes and picks her phone to inform the same at her workplace

Do you wish to go for a holiday Angie for 3 days and then we can come
back and resume our offices and after office, we can spend time at your place so where do you want me to take you if I assume that's a yes from your end?
Angie is astonished- when did you plan all this? Anyway lets go to beachside place and remember the rest of the remaining days is not about you and me it's about us so I would like to take the privilege to give you all you desire... let's do something let us write our desires on a page for this trip and hand over to each other ? What do you think?
I think it's a perfect idea…just as perfect as you are my love
I know it's difficult to understand but I do get it that you have not to lead
a happy life too; you too need love with the same intensity as I need It...
I love you Keith and I can never imagine you as a depressed person … I
will break down much earlier if you break down …
Alright, Angie … let's go packing …
Yes but before that don't you think we should book the tickets and hotels prior to that we should know where are we going?
Yes, you have a point – let's go Mauritius?
What? Are you serious?
Yes absolutely
Alright, then I am booking the tickets and hotel…
(Post 15 minutes on phone)
Our flight is at midnight…
So let's finish packing and go bank once for cash said, Angie Tickets booked,

hotel booked …arrangements done.., bank work is done

and butterflies oh they are having a feast inside us…

As they were traveling towards the airport they remembered their first trip together, the excitement, fear, consciousness …everything was the same

Keith- Angie they both turned at the same time to start a conversation…

Angie Laughed- you start Keith say what you had to

I was wondering if you want me to stop at a medical if requirements are

there … ha-ha

Well that's up to you I am carrying my medical requirements as in my medicines... ha-ha

After Airport arrival and formalities they boarded the flight and a long-awaited trip starts … they're holding hands watching a movie on the go…and lots of cuddling up

The vacation starts…

14. ROMANCE IN THE AIR

As soon as they arrive … it conveys the impression of 'romance in the air'… the weather was amazingly pleasant

They book a cab for the hotel- at the reception, Keith was astonished to

hear his name- as the receptionist called out -Mrs. and Mr. Angie… you're key

Like really Angie - you booked it on this name??

Yes- since right now someone already is mrs.keith I booked it on my name … why do you dislike it?

No- not at all- I am too happy to be called that ….

Okay then let me take you to the ride of your life

Ahem Ahem! I am scared …. Hahaha

You should be - with a blushing smile

As they entered the room it had about 10 sticky notes on the door - which was the to-do list of the day … like each note had a hidden task which Keith had to do if he wants to sleep in the same room-

Too maniacal …right? Lol.

Indeed it is -

By the time they reach the hotel, it was quite late… so they settled their

luggage and slept ...as soon as Keith came beside Angie and took the blanket she said to be ready for your to-do list tomorrow.

By all means mam!

Since it was quite late, they decided on the same – let's change into something comfortable and .... Sleep...said Keith...

Why did you take a pause after let's change into something comfortable....?? Said, Angie

I mean a little bit of cuddling can take place between these two activities

... right? Said, Keith

Right...said Angie...

As they were lying beside each other with Angie half tilted towards Keith's shoulder....

Keith...is this true? Are we really living this??

Yes, Angie... we are living this... and if everything goes well we will always live this...

Angie had a drop of tear in her left eye... Keith doesn't give me hopes on something you know you might never be able to give me...

I have had nightmares about our separation and I have died a million times living the same day you left me, again and again, every night....

I do not have anything to prove you my love Angie but I do know... that

you are all my heart wants... and I would do anything needed to keep my heart safe this time...

I love you, Angie...I always have been in love with you and I always will... I do not know what tomorrow holds for us but I do know that we

will be holding each other's soul for life...

No matter how unfair life was with us... or maybe it will be... but our love is more than just fair... today I want to promise you, Angie, you will be my first thought when I wake up and last thought when I am going to sleep... even if after the remaining days we part ways I will be

yours forever…and even if we do not part ways I am yours forever…. I
belong to you Angie and you belong to me…
Keith, I always have a hard time saying exactly what I feel … I end up saying things that are irrelevant but I do want to try saying…
I Love you too Keith – more than the word love itself, more than I could
ever love myself, more than the possibilities and more than the unfair part we have been through… I do not know what will happen after the
remaining days but I do know….Keith … you are not only my love of life but you are also the sole reason for my existence… I consider you as
my husband from the day you proposed me to be your girl… and no matter if it's not legal... But I am your first wife…
I know this time your intentions are pure… I know this time you won't
leave me just like that…
I trust you with my life, Keith… I love you with all I have…
With these small conversations, they soon slept ….

15. FAIRYTALES HAVE AN END

The next morning was more like a dream both of them were dying to live....you know the most powerful strength booster is lying beside the love of your life and knowing you have them for forever... well in their case it wasn't really like the forever kinds but seeing each other and being around was much more than they expected... the hope of it was almost dead but what we say is somehow true cause destiny had other plans for them....

As Angie got up she came closer to Keith's face kissed his forehead and uttered no matter what the future holds for us, no matter how the course

of love will take us.... I will love you now and till my last breath... and if there is life after death, even after that I will love you always ...

Keith opens his eyes had a glimpse of her holds her in his arms and says

I haven't seen a more beautiful morning than this ... thank you so much

for making my life worth living.... Mmmmm....The Cuddling went a bit

longer than usual... in between Angie crops up with a statement - your to-do list starts now.... So according to the first chit, you will have to start the morning with controlling your emotions- lol- I will seduce you

but you can't react....neither can you touch me ....

What are you nuts?? Said Keith .... Why are you doing this to me early

in the morning can we do this later??
No way this is what the first chit is about … you have to do this….
Alright!! Help me, God!!
Here have a seat - Angie pulled a chair in front of the bed … Keith sits on the chair - Angie is sitting right opposite to him on the bed …. She placed her right leg on Keith's shoulder moves it all around him...from his neck to his waist …. She then got down from the bed and placed her
right hand inside Keith's T-shirt from behind… kisses him all over from
his ears to the neck...shoulders… Keith is almost losing his sense and unable to control the urge of touching her as soon as he moves his hand
back to hold her she moves away and starts laughing -
Why are you laughing Angie?? Because you lost in completing the first chit… lol and I was sure you would fail….that's why…
Very funny - Keith uttered looking annoyed …
Now let's get ready so that we can explore something outside the hotel -
No way- more 9 chits are due and before that, you can't leave the room -
said Angie…
What all 9?? Right now?? Keith said looking shocked
Yes, my love...right now -
Fine - let's start, what more have you planned to make me uncomfortable
….
Awww don't be annoyed love …all the other chits except the last one are

easy...

Hmmm, let's see how easy they are...

The second chit demanded 100 kisses for Angie only on the face except for the lips...

Interesting this one seems to be in my favor said Keith...as he holds Angie makes her sit on the bed and start the kisses...

During the opening of the third chit - Keith's phone rings it was his wife

- he decides to reject the call, and moves toward Angie for the third chit... it said he needs to give 7 promises which he would not break ever...

Just when he was about to start the promises - his wife calls him up again- Angie moves towards him and softly said ... please attend maybe

it's something urgent ....

He picks up the call and his wife started crying - Keith - Githa is in hospital ... doctors have suspected she has acute asthma ... she needs you if you can please come ...

What?? When did this happen and why are you telling me now - am coming ASAP. Meanwhile, call Ryan (Ryan was her best friend and ex and Keith was aware of their secret relation till now) as he stays nearby...

He keeps the phone inside his pocket turned towards Angie and says ...

we need to leave Angie - I am so sorry but Githa needs me ....it's okay Keith! I understand let's leave ...

16. THE WAIT

You know the worst part about waiting is that you don't really know whatever you are waiting for will happen or not … but there aren't many
options and waiting is all you have…
You know sometimes waiting is better than the end of wait… because it's filled with hope … but once it ends it ends…
Angie must have picked up her phone to call Keith 100 times in the last
2 days but not once she had the courage to talk… she decides to stop by
Keith's house just in the hope to see him once...As she gets ready to leave … she thinks ...what if I see him with his wife ??… I don't think I
can ever see him with another woman… What if he seems happier with
his child??
Arghhh … she covers both her ears with her hands and forces herself to
stop thinking …
She gathers the courage and reaches outside Keith's house… He was playing with Githa on the lawn outside his house…
Angie was starring only him from behind a car parked bang opposite to
his house premises … then suddenly she notices-
He is seeming as happy with Githa as he stays with me … how can I

even think of doing this to such a little girl who will always be in dilemma- what was she punished for??

NO!! I can't do this .... But I can't survive without Keith ... I love him!!

I need to ... she is thinking and her mind and heart are totally at war...

Alright, I will stick to my plan - I will not spoil this family - I will leave on the 13th day - (that is if Keith will come back to complete the promise he made ...)

With a sadness that can't be described, she decides to leave ... as soon as

she stops a cab - she turns and looks at Keith who was holding Githa in

his arms... and utters to herself - To love is human to be loved is divine -I hope I see you again my love - and that I can be blessed to spend one

last night with you that will make up for the rest of my life!! I love You, Keith ... I Love You Madly ... So much that I am leaving you for you!!

Wipes her tears that were rolling down - and sits in the cab ....

Meanwhile, Keith holding Githa in his arms - had tears in her eyes ... he

is feeling bad that he hasn't called Angie for 2 days... as soon as Githa fell asleep - he covers her with a blanket and quickly pics up his phone to call Angie -

22 missed calls but Angie wasn't receiving the calls... where the hell is she - is she okay?? Keith is thinking and going paranoid - I hope she has

not done something to herself- suddenly the phone rings and it's a message from Angie -

Sorry I was taking a shower ... say

Pheww I got scared, Angie - replied Keith

Don't be - I am okay - hows Githa?

Why are you talking in this way- are you upset with me??

Why should I be?

Because I didn't call you from past 2 days

LOL- nice at least you know what you did...

I am sorry Angie I was just too blank to think anything .... I will come to see you about 7 ... is it okay??

Yes, and I am not mad at you.... There is a difference between angry and hurt - (this was the last message from Angie for the day)

Angie spends the whole day in restlessness ... there wasn't a single corner of her house left where she didn't hide from her thoughts... her mental inability to recover was topping up the situation...

The doorbell rings ...

Suddenly the excitement was turned into fear of losing each other - Keith on another side of the door was thinking to take Angie home to Githa with a fear that will it go well... and Angie on another side was thinking that it's almost impossible for her to let him go after 13 days but she has to...

She opens the door - they both hug ... the hug was different from the rest of the days... it was tighter - because the love was taken over by fear of losing each other...

Come said, Angie - holding his hand tighter than ever... on the verge of

crying...

As soon as the door closes - they hug again and Angie couldn't control her tears- she holds the collar of Keith's shirt tightly and questions- didn't you miss me once in these 2 days?? Can you live without me? If you can live for 2 days maybe you can survive more days … why Keith?? Why are you doing this to me?? She couldn't even breathe properly- she was on her knees crying out loud …

Keith was shocked seeing her in this condition - as Angie suffered a problem that she can't cry in front of anyone - she has a problem of speaking opposite of what she wants when she is in pain

And always had a guard to her pain so that no one can touch it … and today she is saying exactly what she desires … and crying?? Keith was emotionally shattered seeing her this way - he picks her up in his arms…

hugs her… tightly - and then starts kissing her madly - her face was covered with a layer of tears - he wiped it with his kisses - carrying her inside the room- made her sit on the bed - and on his knees, he took out

a ring from his pocket and proposed Angie for marriage…

17. THE PROMISES AND THE PROPOSAL

Angie – I am here on my knees

I want to confess that I am madly in love with you, it started with a huge

crush … but I knew it there and then that this was special… you make me weak and give me strength at the same time… I am crazy over you…all I know when I am up and I all my dreams are about am our love our togetherness…

I was stupid enough to let you go earlier… I was stupid enough to think

that I can survive without you…. I was stupid enough to doubt your love… but I don't want to be stupid anymore… I want to rectify all my

mistakes and make it extra special for you this time….

I am sorry Angie for making you this way; because of me, you have gone silent… my super talkative girl turned into a silent matured one… I

have no clue how isolated you have made yourself and how did you survive all these years but I want to know about every day you were in pain, about every incident that took place … about every change you forcefully applied on yourself… I want to know this new Angie too and

love her even more…

I want to be there for you when you wake up from a nightmare… I want

to hold you so tight that you never feel alone even in your dreams…I want to make breakfast for you, go for movies …drives… and that crazy
conditions you put on me in the form of paper chits….
I want you to remember whatever happened and not forgive me just because you love me… I want you to just give me a chance to prove that
this time nothing will go wrong…. And if it does I will never leave you alone to suffer….
So Miss. Angie… would you give me the privilege of being your partner
for the rest of our lives?
Angie will you marry me please and make me the luckiest guy on earth….
Will you accept me as a companion and let me shower you with all the love I have
Well, it's nothing in comparison to how deeply affectionate you are about me but I do want to show you how special and how loved you are…
So Angie …. Will you marry me and become Mrs. Keith for life???

18. ACCEPTANCE

You know - the happiness of getting something you thought you have lost is happier than the happiness you have hoped for…

No - Keith you can't do this to Githa especially she…

Shhhhh Angie - I have planned everything …

But I just want to know from you - would you accept my proposal with

a 2 and half-year-old kid ??

Will you accept Githa in our lives???

What??? What about your wife??

She is dating her friend Ryan … I have been speaking to her for the past

2 days that's the reason I didn't call you… Last night she told me she will be more than happy to separate from me and she doesn't want Githa

as well… but for now, she cannot go ahead with divorce proceedings she

needs time for that …

I … I just can't believe this Keith … are you serious?? Angie was trying hard not to lose her mind - she was that happy … but somehow she wasn't being able to trust whatever was happening …

Angie - I thought a lot - I put myself in weird situations - I have lost everything I loved … and in the process of social customs and culture, I

lost my self-happiness too… I want it back - I want to grow old with you

Angie - I want to spend my entire life with you - I have this ring with me
ever since we started dating - and today I am not only giving this ring to
you but am also handing you with the happiness you deserve - you have
waited for me long enough … I am yours … only yours from now till forever … let us start with "our" forever - with something you always wanted out of me - "commitment " - we are getting married after 4 days
… I have prepared everything - I am shifting to your house the day after
our marriage … and I Love You, Angie !!

Unable to digest whatever happened Angie had a panic attack … she collapsed … Keith rushes her to the hospital…

As the doctors take her inside the examination room Keith had tears in
his eyes - he folds his hands look above and prays - God please she is all
I have please make her fine …

Half an hour passed by -

As soon as the doctor came outside the examination room - Keith rushed
to him and asked in a disturbed voice - is she okay?? What is it?

Relax you have to keep yourself calm - she is absolutely okay and a person suffering from schizophrenia can…

Wait ...what is she suffering from?? Asked Keith

Schizophrenia - she has schizophrenia … don't you know that?? Are you

related to her or can you call someone who is aware of this?
Keith was shattered … he looked at the doctor with tears
Doctor, she has been living alone for 8 years...there is no one who is aware of this, I am her would-be husband ...so you can brief me about it…
That's quite strange - it could have been too dangerous - the only cure to
this is love and regular medicines ...anyway as you are going to be her husband… make sure she is attending counseling - having medicines on
time and love should be the priority
Love - I am her love doctor and I am her illness … I made her this way … and I will get her back…
That's good nodded the doctor but remember never trust her with her words even if she is saying okay … follow the doctor's instruction ….
Before taking any major steps …
Take care and have a happy married life …
Can I see her doctor??
Yes, go ahead …
As he entered the room -you scared me Angie for the first time … you scared me … we have been meeting and spending time and you kept me
so away from you even after being so near to you … maybe I deserve it…
But, let's forget all this - and concentrate on our marriage … (just to divert her mind)
Yes - let us said Angie in a soft voice - thank you, Keith … I almost gave up on us this time… I was about to leave you uninformed … but you got us back together … and yes… I have a ring too for you- opens

her locket and there was a ring in it...which she was wearing from the day she got separated … it had Keith written on it… I Love You!!
And as I accept Githa with us - you accept my Schizophrenia??
Will you??
Already have!!
You know the most beautiful thing about love is- that no matter how
immense pain it caused you - when it's favorable - it can be the reason to live a happy life… No matter how many big hurdles life throws at you - Love can conquer it with grace …
For me, Keith and Angie were meant to be together - it was like their souls was connected in an inseparable way … the hearts were separate but it beat as one … moreover, they were incomplete without each other …
"Whatever it may be wherever I am - I am all about you, just like people
have surnames - YOU ARE MY IDENTITY"

Printed by Libri Plureos GmbH in Hamburg,
Germany